CONVERSATIONS

Julia Duke

Conversations

© Julia Duke

First Edition 2021

Julia Duke has asserted her authorship and given her permission to Dempsey & Windle for these poems to be published here.

Photograph of the author by Douglas Duke

Published by Dempsey & Windle
15 Rosetrees
Guildford
Surrey
GU1 2HS
UK
01483 571164
dempseyandwindle.com

A catalogue record for this book is available from the British Library

British Library Cataloguing-in-Publication Data

ISBN: 978-1-913329-58-7

Printed and bound in the UK

'all real living is meeting'

Martin Buber

CONTENTS

Foreword:

'Conversations' is the culmination of a life-time's digging into the whole issue of human 'connectedness' and intimacy. Experiences of childhood bullying led me to ask deep questions about the ways in which relationships, good and bad, dominate our lives and are responsible for so much of our sense of wellbeing and mental health. Family, school, 'house church' and working relationships informed my thinking until, as a mature student at Sussex University in the 90's, I came across the writings of a Jewish philosopher and poet, Martin Buber.

Born in Vienna, Buber was abandoned by his mother when still very young and spent his life developing ideas of 'meeting' and 'mis-meeting', a word he invented to describe his own emotion at the dysfunctional nature of failed family relationships. His philosophical writings divide human relationships into 'I-Thou': a state of intimacy and single-minded focus and 'I-It': a less elevated, less intense, but more functional state of connection. For Buber, I-It formed the basis of routine communication for the purposes of information, entertainment, instruction or day-to-day casual connection but without the intimacy of the I-Thou relationship. Without that intimacy, taught Buber, no real meeting of minds and hearts could occur. His small volume of autobiographical writings was entitled simply 'Meetings' and consisted of a series of personal stories in the Jewish Hasidic tradition that documented his own search for closeness and belonging.

In 'Conversations' I take my own look at meetings and mis-meetings. The poems question whether the combination of our busy, modern lives and our habitual uprootedness threatens both the art of communication and the affirming experience of being rooted and grounded in communities. Writing and putting together 'Conversations' has been a way of scratching the 'itch' that has dogged me for a number of years.

Julia Duke

Firstborn

The pram wheels sink deep in fresh, soft snow;
sky of baby blue. This January boy seems apt,
designed for crisp perfection:
unsullied, pristine, sparkling,
like the watery Geneva sunshine.
Everything whispers 'new'.

Drinking in my star-struck wonder,
marinated in love, returning my gaze
without missing a beat —
not a hint of suspicion.
Soft, white, baby-fresh,
your world is simple,
your needs are few.

In your world the closest attention
is paid to the tiniest of details:
a small fleck of yellow sleep
brushed from your eye;
the tiniest of milk spots
brooded over anxiously;
at feeding time, around your lips,
a tiny tinge of blue.

Heart-rending tears,
followed by utter contentment.
Fast asleep now, little one,
tiny cheek on tiny hand, breathing
deep, deep sighs of satisfaction.
Tiptoe softly around him
lest you waken this blissful repose.
Once this was you.

Food, warmth, the touch of a hand,
a sense of belonging,
the simple joy of being loved,
and human contact, eye to eye,
unashamed, unblinking.
Somewhere down the line
we strayed and lost our way.
How we never knew.

Neighbourhood Gossip

After 'Neighbourhood Gossip' by Honoré Daumier (1855)

Before these women's candour
even the sun's ardour pales,
unable to match their energy
before it sinks beneath the hills
and the world is put to rights.

Here is guileless gossip
(we are eavesdropping on
intimate conversation)
that defines boundaries,
makes judgements,
heals wounds,
brings us together.

This is the stuff the world is made of:
humanity oozes from every pore.
A gentle colour wash,
a few sharp outlines
traced in black;
a message clear to all:
a rural community,
viewed through the eyes of a child.

For their eyes are watching,
watching every move,
innocent eyes
learning how the world revolves,
how the world works,
what makes it tick.

'It takes a whole village
to bring up a child.'
A whole village to instil wisdom,
nurture and inspire,
a whole village
wrapped
in an embrace
that includes us all.

Beneath the shadow
of this tree
a family is forged.
Beneath the shelter
of this tree
a community is built.
Daumier understood.

Champagne Cocktails

It was on the billboard:
Fizzy Friday,
with small print underneath
inviting us to sip champagne.
A nice way of spending Friday.

'You need life experience,' he said,
'before you bring someone else
into this world.'
A wise head on young shoulders.
'Don't bring a baby into this world, not yet.'

The young man held forth -
'Champagne cocktails,' he said,
mentioning the Ritz,
the Waldorf, tantalising stuff.
A nice way of spending any day.

They talked of jobs, of uni,
'I'm going to be, like, thirty-five
before I can have kids'
she said. 'A job's a job,
but I wanted more.'

'He's changed a lot from High School!'
She can't say how - 'it's personal.'
'I thought he'd give me a lift home:
twenty-five quid for a taxi!'
A nice way of spending a fortune.

'You have to dress up smart,'
he said. (We never did.)
Their lives stretched ahead
full of serious stuff
and a lot of fizzy Fridays.

'I get very merry' she said.
'I hit my head - it bled
and they called an ambulance.'
'It's a funny old world,' I said.
'I've never spent a fizzy Friday.'

Ennui

After 'Ennui' by Walter Sickert (c.1914)

Gone, long gone, vanished in the autumn fog
that crept insidiously, wound itself
like a scarf around the throat,
a smouldering flame
that once burned bright, fluttered,
then guttered.

As passion wanes, the flickering memories
yield a careworn, hollow shell,
a winter's discontent. Gaze
at faded, yellow walls,
inhale the musty, soured smell
of a hundred spent cigars.

The spark they once had known was done,
snuffed out. No-one noticed; no-one cared.
The moment passed them by,
unmourned and unrepented.
Too late for tears, recriminations,
much too late for reparations.

The Wrestlers
After 'Wrestlers' lino-cut, Henri Gaudier-Brzeska (c.1914)

Intimacy hovers, poised at the point of a knife:
the artist's decision, skilful incision, will shape
the outcome of this skirmish. When a scuffle
breaks out among boys, who knows
where it will end.

No easy brush strokes; each cut made with purpose.
Each thrust of the knife a new thrust
in their struggle. Each twist of the torso
a deep violation, a mute exhortation,
a tentative knowing.

Interwoven, interlocking, grasping and gasping,
panting and rasping, poised on the cusp
of success, almost basking,
then a plunging, sudden lunging,
interlinking, almost sinking.

Blood runs deep. It's thicker than water.
They grapple and tussle, inextricable tangle,
convolution of limbs, a contortion, a wrangle.
Caught up with each other in
search of a brother.

Monday Morning Café

Maniacal laughter
ruptures my solitude,
grates on my ear.

Scrapes, scars,
scours, scratches,
wounding my soul.

Her words stutter,
judder like a machine gun.
His words hit the floor.

His gentle interjections
soothe to no avail.
She is invincible.

Never stopping for breath,
she is learning her trade:
learning to teach on the job.

I am at a loss. How will she
learn anything? Conversation:
a one-way street.

I feel for her students.
The voice grinds on,
punctuated by staccato laughter.

I am imprisoned,
regressing to school days:
those Friday afternoons,

trapped in the classroom,
crushed by expectations,
longing for home…

No longer a child,
I resist, slowly lean back
in my chair.

Suddenly
she's gone
and my thoughts are my own.

This Is Not About the Robin

He is a brooding restlessness in the garden.
Installed in the corner, he leans, self-absorbed,
across a table full of guests
trying in vain to continue their conversation.

The speckled robin is trapped, bewildered,
at the mercy of his telephoto lens,
separated from its mother by this tall stranger
who towers over his victim, intent on his obsession.

We, his audience, are captivated, caught in his spell.
We watch, fascinated, yet secretly despising
his overbearing manner. A man with a mission,
he reduces us to a passive role. We are mere tourists.

The woman sits, unmoved by his antics.
They are husband and wife; she knows him well.
A solid presence, she presides over the tea-table,
but like a wilful child, he will not sit down.

The robin has fled, seeking refuge in the lilac.
He approaches stealthily, stalking it with his lens.
Skulking in the shadows, helpless, its mother
hovers nearby, eyes bright with fear.

A brief interlude; he devours his scone,
fiddles with his camera, gulps his tea.
The study in blue who sits at his side
ignores him. There is nothing left to say.

He glances around, fidgets, stacks the cups,
arranging them on the tray. Swiftly
he carries them indoors. Teatime is over.
I watch them in silence, making up stories.

This is not about the robin. A mere bit part:
its task is done. The real drama, I see it now,
continues much later, behind closed doors:
two starring roles battling it out for supremacy.

Collaboration

I begin my sentence with hesitation,
cautiously I knit words together,
build logic, tying my thoughts neatly,
advancing towards an obvious conclusion.

He interrupts, forestalls me,
mistaking hesitation for failing speech,
offering an unwanted solution,
helping an old lady across a road
she never wanted to cross.

Patiently, I unpick his words,
resentful of this unsolicited collaboration.
Now my task is doubled; unpicking done,
I must begin again.

Portrait of the Artist's Wife

After 'Portrait of the Artist's Wife' Henri Matisse (1913)

Her husband has her well-trained.
She knows how to dress.
Stylish, she sits erect, head tilted,
with a patient, knowing smile.
She's in for the long haul.

The perfect colour match:
a silky, pea-green blouse simpers
beneath her turquoise tailored jacket
with its black velvet lapels.
Her right arm drapes the wooden chair.

Outlined in black her eyebrows arch.
Her eyes are dark, inscrutable,
her nose neat, her lips thin, determined.
Her head is crowned by the sweetest of hats,
black, chic, with a pink rose.

Against a vivid, peacock blue screen
Madame Matisse is beguiling. It's perfect,
save the artist's final stroke of genius
(that telling use of complementary colours):
a golden scarf wound about her shoulders.

They are an accomplished pair,
the artist and his wife; his skill, her charm,
entwined forever. This portrait shows it well.
Half a lifetime of complementary giftings:
a marriage made on the colour wheel of heaven.

Body Language

After 'Conversation' by Henri Matisse (1908-12)

He's seen that look before,
takes him right back:
didn't mean to be late,
knew the drill,
home by ten-thirty
sharp.

Caught in a scrap,
missed the bus home.
Ran all the way
skirting the park.
Facing his mother,
covers his tracks,
fingering the pack of Woodbine
in his pocket.

In her elegant gown his wife sits
erect, chin tilted,
dark hair swept back,
pert, so full of questions,
early in the morning,
watching his face turn
a dark red.

Counting the hours, waiting up,
does she guess where he's been?
He stands tall,
looks her in the eye.
Maybe it's about his pyjamas;
the blue and white stripe
doesn't turn her on.

.

Psychobabble for Beginners

I had a friend once, a powerful woman, Heenti,
with an accent that clung like thick porridge,
despite seventeen years in my homeland that failed
to change her stubborn Dutch intonation.

Forcefully, with utter sincerity, she urged:
'Don't ask why'. 'Why not?' I asked instinctively.
'Just don't *ask*' she said. 'Why?' I asked again.
She accused me of 'negatism'. I let it pass.

Julia was a different kettle of fish. On the lookout
for trainee clients, she liked a chance to practise.
My weekly visits on the tram buoyed me up no end,
gave me hope, refreshed my questioning mind.

Julia said I needed to trust. By this time I had
let go my childish faith - I guess because
I used the why word too many times. Trust what? I asked.
'Trust in the process' she said. I'm still thinking about that.

'Don't look back', they say. 'Just move on.' Lot's wife
stumbled badly over that one, froze in her tracks, exceeded
the recommended limit of sodium chloride. A worthy mantra,
but the escape route out of Sodom's not so popular these days.

Don't mess with my head, friends. It's attached to my heart,
a holistic minefield, it seems, where trouble brews,
regrets fester, doubts linger. Mine have a life
all their own. They multiply like question marks.

Should Auld Acquaintance...

I am replete. Wined and dined,
that warm feeling churning
in the pit of my stomach,
I ponder old friendships,
the ones that remain.

They have stood the test of time,
enfolding me again
in that remembered embrace,
reassuring me that all is well.

I am empowered. The healthy balance
that accrued through the sharing
of our lives has endured. Warmed
by your affection, I am secure.

We have come from different lands,
travelled by different paths,
but here, for a short, precious time
our paths have crossed. Now,
returning, we feast upon those moments,
remember our shared history.

After all these years apart, it is
still the same. Old friends are like that.

Delft, Netherlands

Doppelganger

Returning here
I find another self.
You have been patient
waiting for me all these years
ready to spring to attention
when required.

All this time, it seems,
you have been strolling along canals,
climbing the little hump-backed bridges,
looking at your feet
lest you should trip on the cobblestones,
waiting till I returned.

Shopping in Albert Heijn is only natural.
The layout is changed
but the choice is the same.
You are at home, filling your basket
with local cheese, dark brown bread
for which I search in vain
in my other life.

Lentebok is in season,
full of light summer freshness.
It is late June. If I crave the rich brown beer of *herfst*
I must return in October. This is how it is done,
always the same. My tongue cannot forget
how to shop in Dutch. Like riding a bike
I will always remember.

In the Saturday market
I meet you at our favourite stall.
Choosing strawberries,
I am greeted like an old friend:
'*Op vakantie?*' she asks.
I smile and nod, tell her
it is good to be back.
And it is.

Morgan Jones Lies Here

Morgan Jones lies here,
marked for eternity since 1824
by a grey slab,
reclining under yellowing turf,
with a view of the sea
to die for.

Lewis Evans, oblivious now,
hidden beneath grey slate
defaced only by lichens,
pale and blotched,
weathered by sea breezes,
rests at ease.

John Williams, once of this parish,
living in Friog,
is deaf to the seagull's cry,
numb to the lashing rain,
buffeting winds
or burning sun.

Far below them,
the waves beat out the time,
pulsating waves,
sand-blasting wind,
little by little,
eroding memories.

William Lewis and Catherine,
Lewis Evans and Elizabeth,
Williams, Edmund, Lewis,
sharing names,
sharing life,
sharing death,

huddled together
in death as in life,
a community of slate,
resilient and brave,
speaking volumes
in the silence.

Grey slate,
purple heather,
bleached stone walls,
soft white lichens,
backdrop for a community's
proud history.

Inside the church,
a remnant gathers still.
Ancient names
etched on pews,
each one his place.
Each one his time.

Llangelynin Churchyard, Gwynedd

Poignant Meeting

A fleeting visit,
we linger over coffee
until we can postpone the moment
no longer.

We must return,
slowly, reluctantly,
each to her own, on opposite sides of the globe,
separate lives.

We were friends,
shared our lives together,
a brief moment in time,
thrown together

from different continents,
different lifestyles.
We were partners in crime,
soul mates.

One last trip. Before what?
The unspoken question
hovers above the coffee cups,
then we part.

Losing Your Balance

We met outside Looseys, close to Christmas.
Sauntering around antiques, in holiday mood,
I was after bargains: novelties, shabby and chic,
cool and cheap, for our new home. Outside
in Magdalen Street, noisy with traffic, she
appeared from a doorway, slid straight into my world,
asking for spare change. I remember it so well,
the uneasy moment and the acrid smell
of exhaust fumes in the air. Her world caught me
off balance. Self-possession stumbled.

I opened my purse, emptied it into her
outstretched hand. She seemed diffident,
disinterested even, just craving warmth,
some human contact, wanting a bit of conversation.
So many questions hovered. How could I
ask her where home was? So vulnerable, young,
she seemed. On the raw side of life and so alone.
I liked her. She wished us a happy Christmas.
'You too' I muttered, lost for words, hating myself.

I think of her often. She walks through
my waking thoughts, hovers in my dreams,
unsettling me. Set adrift, younger than my daughter,
so small and slight in a thin coat and dress.
Does she have a home, a mother? I think of her now,
the streets virus cleansed. And her future?
Promises fade in a smokescreen of lies.
When it's all over, we'll have 'lessons to learn'.
When we're shopping again might we meet,
back in her doorway, our worlds still self-distanced?

Sweet Conversation

Strategically placed at the corner,
I await their arrival.
They will come together;
they always do.
A lifetime of friendship
has rendered them inseparable
as they process down the street,
two by two, arm in arm.

Engaged in conversation,
focused on staying upright,
they teeter on ill-advised heels,
elegant to the last.
Only Wyn stares ahead of her,
spies me waiting, peers at me.
'Is that Julie?' A cry of welcome
that takes me back: a mother's cry.

Fourteen years since last I heard it,
that spontaneous cry,
like a child's, full of joy,
never failing in warmth:
'Always pleased to see you'.
Now long gone, I remember
with pleasure being enfolded
in the circle of her love.

In the café we sit in a circle
piling sugar crystals
on mugs of foaming coffee,
taking our turn, in deep debate,
drawing warmth, finding joy
from one another's lives.
These days families live so far apart,
estranged, bereaved,

adopting where they can:
other people's mothers,
other people's daughters.
Here we sit together,
piling words on words,
a tiny community brought together
by necessity, like need,
the mother of invention.

First Impressions

My mother read to me in sleepy afternoons,
while my sister was at school. Noddy, Big Ears
— I hated them. Little Grey Rabbit I loved.
Knew them backwards, word for word.
While mother dozed, I prodded, nudged,
so she would finish, so I could hear again
those precious words I longed for.

My mother read to me in sleepy afternoons,
but my father, home from work, would sit me
on his knee, would tell me of his favourite,
told me how the brave and reckless hare
played noughts and crosses with the fox
(O brave and reckless hare!).
Hare's Great Adventure, all my days,
was stamped upon my soul.

Enigma

(i)

Even the sails turn. I still have it,
my first grown-up jewellery
given by my father, thinking of me, while he vanished
on a business trip to Holland. Tiny, perfectly formed
silver windmill: a love gift.

(ii)

After the funeral in 1992, turning out his desk
(most prized possession except for his Books),
I found a small dagger, silver, engraved with camels,
dhows and a rose pattern, broken off at the end,
oozing romance: a tale of Arabian nights
from six years in wartime Baghdad. Such mystery,
intrigue at the heart of an ordinary man's life.
Now it lives in my desk. Why did he go there?

(iii)

The father I knew was an educationalist,
an Oxford man: historian, classicist,
starched collar, clean shirt every day,
dark tie, grey suit, bang on time
(I always kept him waiting);
a stuffed shirt kind of man…

(but you were kind).

He once said he liked Nana Mouskouri;
we still have the L.P. You could have
knocked me down with a feather.

(iv)

I failed at school. Passed my exams brilliantly
and then failed   to follow his tradition
of scholarship, university, intellectualism.
I did other things I wanted more.

Late developer,
a 'mature student', I discovered red brick Sussex.
Rita was finally educated.

(v)

When he had no further need of education
he promised me his books. I asked him why and he said
simply 'because you read them — no-one else does.'
At last a love we shared, something to talk about
as he grew old. The dark green cover of his *Ulysses*
haunts me now, signature on the flyleaf, 'August 1944'.

One thousand pages plus,
to trace a convoluted day's journey
to a failed epiphany that led them to a cup of cocoa
and a mis-meeting; a story that led *me* to the bloom
of a new relationship with that other Stephen
who left me his books (because I read them)
and his absence, an ever-present imperfection
in my graduation (1993 at the Brighton Centre)
that Photo Shop can never rectify. There we stand,

                together, caught unawares,
        'proud Mum'   and me,
    with a wistful look in   our eyes. It was
'in the lap of the gods'   he said, how
my degree turned out.   It turned out well
as it happens...
                except he wasn't there.

Mind the Gap

Inspired by Michelangelo, 'Creation of Adam',
Sistine Chapel ceiling (1508-12)

That tiny gap, we mark it well
(his centrepiece):
two hands reach out,
two lives impinge,
two worlds collide.

A reaching out from time and space
with limitless potential -
that breath of God,
the power of touch -
so 'man' becomes a 'living soul'.

Heart in mouth, anticipate
that crucial spark,
a lightning strike
that could ignite the human race,
could make it fully human.

That tiny gap, we mark it well
(our focal point):
the hands reach out,
a cry for reciprocity
that echoes through eternity.

About the Author

Julia Duke is a poet whose writing is informed by her love of landscape and her fellow humans. Fascinated by all kinds of connections and borders, whether between individuals or nations, Julia has lived in and been inspired by a variety of European locations and their inhabitants. Her working life has been varied, ranging from library work to the setting up of a charity dedicated to international reconciliation and the overseeing of a telephone helpdesk for English-speaking expatriates in the Netherlands. Home for Julia and her husband is currently in Suffolk, after fifteen years in the Netherlands, followed by six on the beautiful west coast of Wales. Their daughter and her family live in Switzerland. Once the travelling bug takes hold of a family it is hard to predict where it will end.

As a writer, Julia loves to experiment. Over the years she has worked extensively at poetry, her first love, and at creative non-fiction, including nature writing, memoir and a recent project on identity. In recent years she has developed her poetry writing more fully, exploring her interest in imagist poetry, free verse and traditional forms such as sonnets, haiku and tanka.

Julia has published a short memoir collection and, while living in the Netherlands, she contributed a weekly column to *The Hague Online*, an English language e-magazine for the expatriate community. She has published a number of poems in anthologies and magazines, including *Fifth Elephant* (anthology of the Newtown Poets), *London Grip* online, Indigo Dreams' magazine *The Dawntreader* and Suffolk Poetry Society's magazine *Twelve Rivers*.

Acknowledgement and Thanks

Thanks are due to Michael Bartholomew-Biggs, for publishing 'The Wrestlers' online in *London Grip New Poetry*, September 2020 issue.

Thanks also go to:

Douglas Duke for his incisive editing skills, awkward questions and endless encouragement; **Chris Kinsey** and **Lara Clough** for their valuable tutoring and unfailing positivity; **The Writers Circle** in The Hague, Netherlands, the **Newtown Writers** and the **Newtown Poets** in Wales and the **Bungay Poetry Café** in Suffolk for their inspiration and encouragement; **The Suffolk Poetry Society** for help and support and a lot of opportunities; **Sue Wallace-Shaddad** for her advice and support; and my publishers at Dempsey & Windle for their efficient and encouraging support through the whole publishing process.